JAVELINA

Have-uh-WHAT?

GENE K. GARRISON

This book was printed in the United States of America.
Second Edition, Revised.

**Acknowledgements: Photos on pages 6, 8, 9, 11, 12, 14,
19, 27, 30, 31, 32, 34 and Photoshop work by Al Brown.
Other photos by the author.**

Dedicated to kids who read

Spiky-looking animals, which look a lot like pigs—
wild ones—are called javelinas.
First, let's pronounce it correctly.
Say *Have-uh-LEE-nah.*
Their scientific name is collared peccary.

Almost salt-and-pepper colored,
with light colored collars,
they look as though someone
started to wash them,
but the clever beasts got away
before the job was done.

They trot about the Sonoran Desert through dry washes on little hooves, past plants with thorns.

Those harsh-looking plants
bud in the springtime.

And before long,
beautiful flowers emerge.

Javelinas live in the southwestern part
of the United States, as well as Mexico
and Central and South America.
The ones we are reading about live
in the Sonoran Desert in Arizona.

The most beautiful parts of it
are full of trees, bushes,
wildflowers and cactus plants,
including the very tall ones with arms,
the saguaro (suh-WHAR-oh).

Pig-faced, with
pink snouts,
javelina eyes don't
see too well—
but their ears
hear splendidly.

They hear every sound—
footsteps making crunching noises
on gravel, squirrels scurrying,
a turtle plodding across the land.
They smell all of these things,
including us.

Pink snouts dip into my little pond, making slurping sounds, and water drips from their mouths back into the pond.

Sometimes they lower themselves
into the water and enjoy a soak.

And when it's time for a nap,
down they flop.

Poppa is the biggest, Mama next in size.
The children look just like their parents, only smaller.
Because we care about them, let's name this
javelina family. How about Boary, Leena,
Piglet, Piggy and Hambone?

They're not much like farm pigs.
The difference is the javelina's tail—it's short,
wide and flat, not a skinny, curly tail.
They have extra-long teeth, called tusks, and they have
stiff hairs, and a gland something like a skunk's.
To us, it smells terrible.

Able to fight if they have to, they scare off enemies by showing their sharp tusks, and by making the bristles on their backs stand straight up, like porcupine spines.

The family members snort gruffly
and bark warnings. After all,
they have to protect each other.

They must watch out for coyotes,
bobcats and mountain lions
who would love a javelina dinner.
It's important that they defend themselves.

Will they bare their ferocious tusks
to scare an intruder away?
Yes, if they sense danger, and they often do.

Boary grunts his orders, and off they run, down dry washes and into the foothills.

Little javelinas know enough to do what their parents say. They represent experience, and that's important, especially when a hungry enemy is in the neighborhood. Nobody wants to become someone else's dinner.

Life is not always dangerous for javelinas.
They live where they want, nibble tasty treats—beans
from the mesquite and palo verde trees, berries,
seeds, and sometimes they push over a barrel cactus
or prickly-pear cactus and eat the roots.
Yummy—for a javelina tummy.

Javelinas aren't the only ones who like the red, pulpy juiciness.

The tiny antelope ground squirrel, and birds, such as the large roadrunner, like them too.

When javelinas eat
the prickly-pear
cactus they'd better
watch out for thorns.

A lot happens in the springtime.

New tender pads appear,
and lovely colorful blossoms burst out.

Stomachs full because of
the generosity of the desert,
javelinas lie down and nap
anywhere they want,
even near my house
in the middle of the day.

But when they raid the garden,
they come at night.

Some people think of them as nuisances,
especially when they dig up flowers
in order to eat the bulbs,
or knock over a cactus for the roots.

They have other endearing traits too.
They scratch where it itches, and wallow in mud puddles
wherever they can find them. Not exactly cuddly-
looking because of their sharp, stiff spikes,
they *are* interesting, in a touch-me-not sort of way.

Watch them from far away.
Don't approach them at all,
but enjoy the presence of a javelina family
trotting on tiny hooves through the desert.

Or maybe you will see dainty javelina tracks, and you will know that they have been there.

Maybe it was the family
who drank from my pond—
Boary, Leena, Piglet, Piggy
and Hambone.
Wouldn't *THAT* be fun?

The End

Vocabulary

Approach (uh-PRO-ch) — to go close to

Blossoms (BLOSS-ums) — flowers

Bristles (BRIS-uls) — short, stiff hairs

Coyotes (KI-oats or Ki-OH-tees) — wild animals that look like small wolves or medium-sized dogs

Critters (KRIT-ers) — small animals, usually wild

Crunching (KRUNCH-ing) — noisy, crisp eating sound

Endearing (en-DEER-ing) — making oneself likable to others

Experienced (x-PEER-ee-enced) — something a person has done or lived through

Ferocious (fer-ROW-shus) — fierce, savage

Generosity (gen-er-AH-suh-tee) — willingness to give

Gruffly (GRUFF-lee) — roughly

Hooves (HOOV-s) — plural of hoof, hard toenail-like feet of horses, cows, sheep, deer and pigs

Intruder (in-TRU-der) — one who goes where he is not wanted

Lush (LUH-sh) — thick, healthy plant growth

Mesquite (mes-KEET) — a desert tree with fern-like leaves

Palo verde (PAL-oh-VER-dee) — sometimes written as one word, it means *green stick* in Spanish. The trunks and branches of these desert trees really are green.

Plodding (PLOD-ing) — walking in a heavy way

Porcupine (PORK-u-pine) — wild animals with quills

Presence (PREZ-ence) — not absent

Pulpy (PUL-pee) — like the soft, juicy part of fruit

Raid (RAYD) — a surprise attack

Represent (rep-ree-ZENT) — to act or speak for

Scurrying (SKUR-ee-ing) — hurrying along

Slurping (SLURP-ing) — a loud sipping sound

Spiky (SPIKE-ee) — pointed

Splendidly (SPLEN-did-lee) — excellently

Trotting (TROT-ing) — stepping along in a peppy way

Tusks (TUSK-s) — long, pointed teeth of some animals

Wallow (WHAL-low) — to settle down in mud

Made in the USA
Las Vegas, NV
15 November 2020